SPOT

MOTORSPORTS

DRAGSTERS

by Alissa Thielges

amicus LEARNING

dragstrip

light stand

Look for these words and pictures as you read.

tire

tailpipe

A car zips by.
It is a dragster.

These cars are super fast. Drivers feel like they are on a rocket.

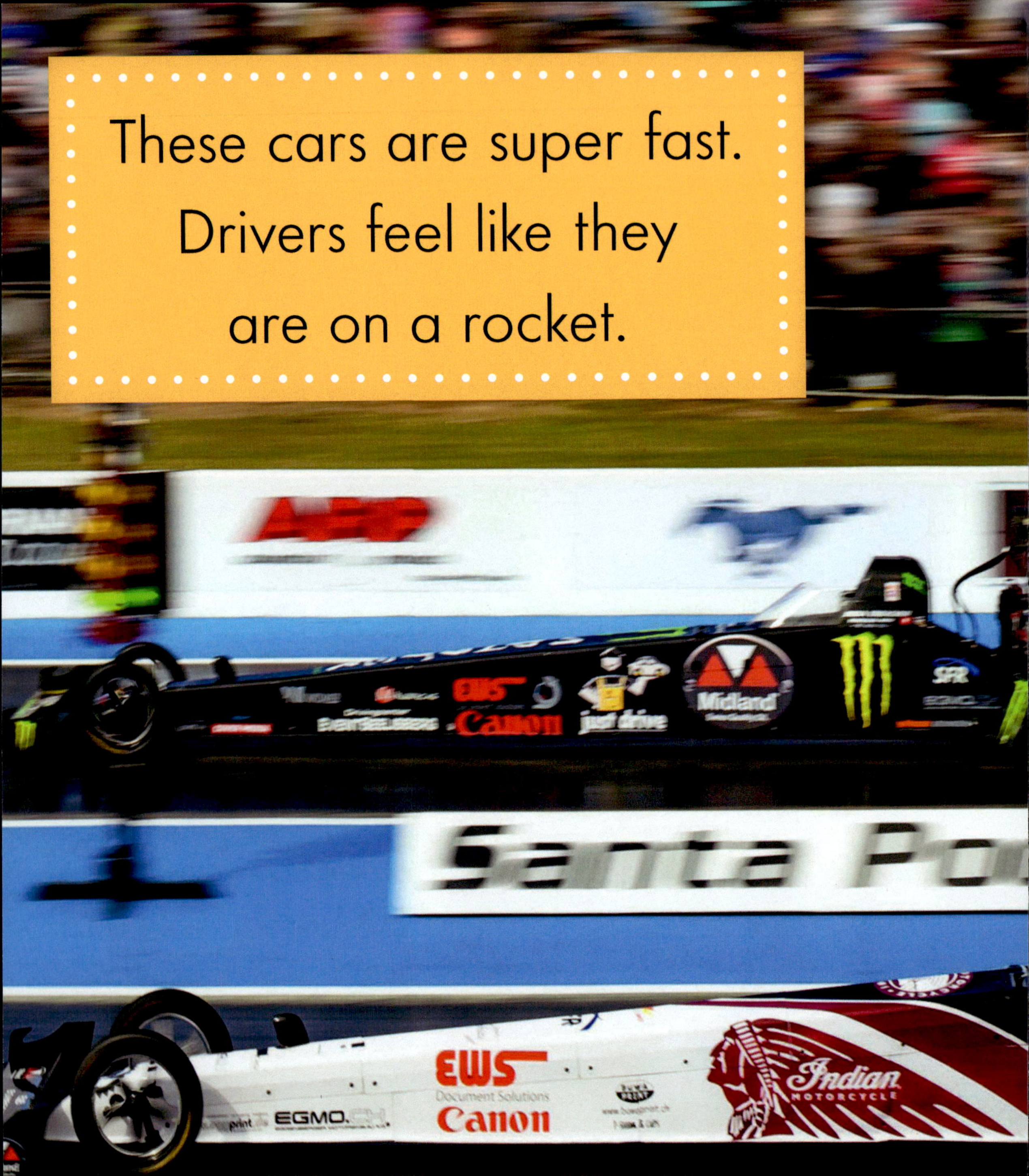

TF
FIA
Midland
Swiss Quality Oil.
COVER MEDIA

SANT
coldfire
firefighting
official partner

dragstrip

See the dragstrip?

It is short.

Cars race on it.

PRE-STAGE
STAGE

light stand

See the light stand?
The lights flash.
Green means go!

See the big tires?
They spin fast.
The rubber burns.

tire

NFC

See the tailpipe?
The fuel burns hot.
It catches on fire!

tailpipe

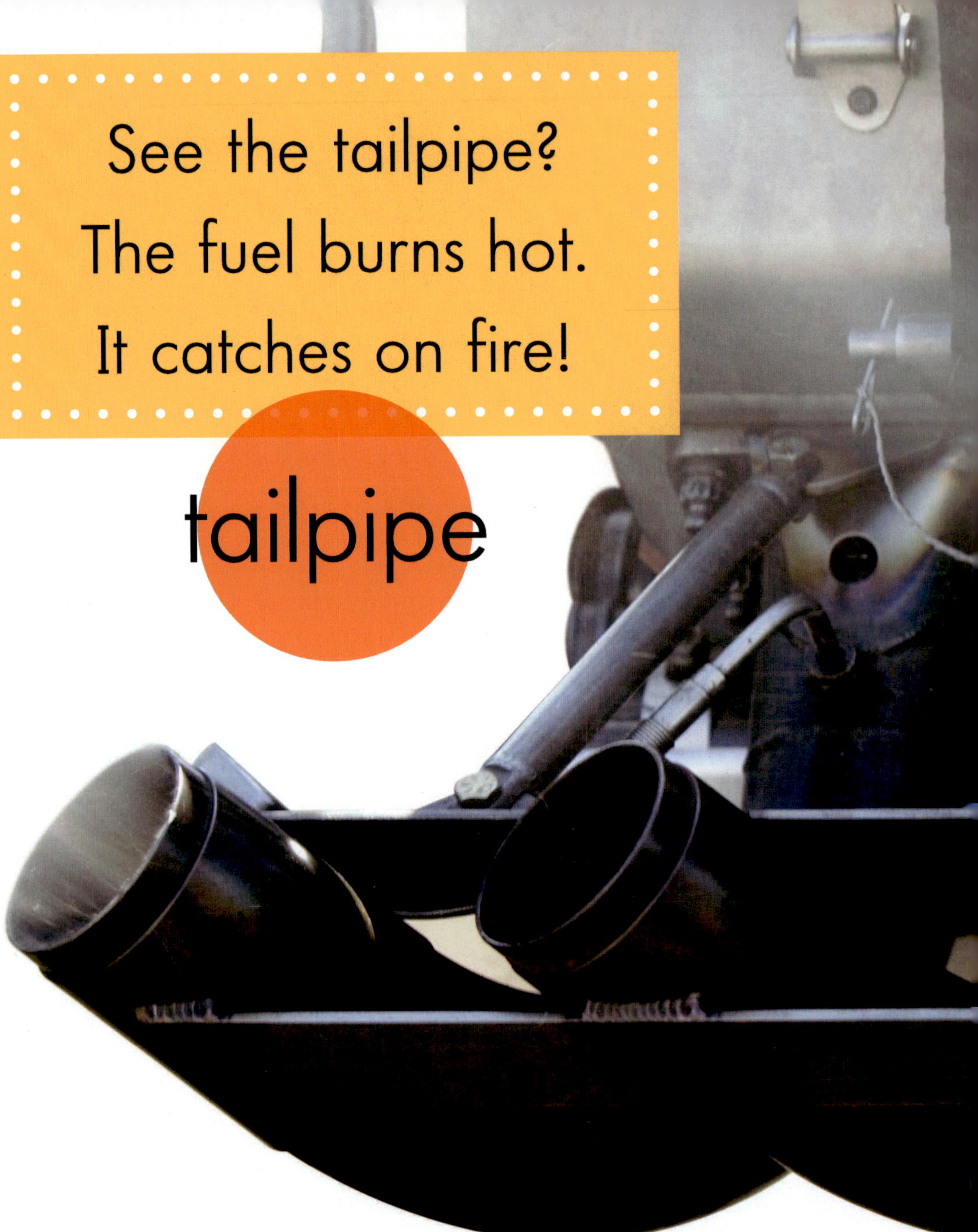

Titanium and Aluminum Performance Products
www.diversatech.com

The dragsters take off.
The race is over in seven seconds!

dragstrip

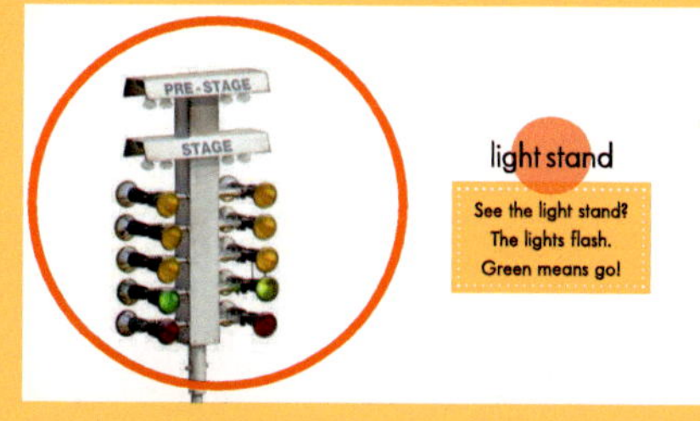

light stand

Did you find?

tire

tailpipe

SPOT

Spot is published by Amicus Learning, an imprint of Amicus
P.O. Box 227, Mankato, MN 56002
www.amicuspublishing.us

Library of Congress Cataloging-in-Publication Data
Names: Thielges, Alissa, 1995- author.
Title: Dragsters / by Alissa Thielges.
Description: Mankato, MN : Amicus Learning, [2026] | Series: Spot motorsports | Audience: Ages 4–7 | Audience: Grades K–1 | Summary: "Dragsters are lightweight race cars known for their wide rear tires and use in drag races. This search-and-find book reinforces new vocabulary words with simple facts and compelling photographs to teach kindergarten readers about motorsports"— Provided by publisher.
Identifiers: LCCN 2024050087 (print) | LCCN 2024050088 (ebook) | ISBN 9798892004817 (library binding) | ISBN 9798892005357 (paperback) | ISBN 9798892005890 (ebook)
Subjects: LCSH: Dragsters—Juvenile literature. | Drag racing—Juvenile literature. | CYAC: Dragsters. | Drag racing.
Classification: LCC TL236.2 .T53 2026 (print) | LCC TL236.2 (ebook) | DDC 629.228/5—dc23/eng/20250110
LC record available at https://lccn.loc.gov/2024050087
LC ebook record available at https://lccn.loc.gov/2024050088

Ana Brauer, editor
Deb Miner, series designer
Sara Hood, book designer and photo researcher

Photos by Alamy Stock Photo/Kelvin Webb, 12–13, Screenbyte, 10–11, Tony Watson, 4–5; Dreamstime/Chris Boswell, 1, G00b, cover; Getty Images/David Allio/Icon Sportswire, 3, Jeff Speer/Icon Sportswire, 14; Shutterstock/Oil and Gas Photographer, 8; Wikimedia Commons/Daniel Smith, 6–7